The Best Family of All

Mary E. LeBar

illustrated by
William Lackey

VICTOR BOOKS

a division of SP Publications, Inc., Wheaton, Illinois
Offices also in Fullerton, California • Whitby, Ontario, Canada • London, England

All Scripture quotations are from the King James Version.

ISBN: 0-88207-251-X

It's wonderful to belong to God's family. It's wonderful to be His very own child. And that wonder has happened to YOU!

It's the best thing that *has* ever happened to you. It's the best thing that *will* ever happen to you even if you grow very tall and very old and very wise and very rich.[1]

When you truly belong to God's family, you belong to the best family of all.

1. How did you get into His family? *Let's remember . . . .*
2. How do God's children grow? *Let's find out . . . .*

Getting into God's Family

     First, God made you . . .
your arms and legs that move, move, move!
Your mouth that likes to make BIG noises,
your hair just the way it is,
your happy smile.
     God made the real YOU that lives inside your body
too, the you that can't have a picture taken—
the you that loves,
the you that hates,
the you that thinks of good answers,
the you that sometimes can't think of anything to say!

But even though God was your Maker,
He wasn't your heavenly Father yet.[2]
　　He couldn't be the heavenly Father of a child
who said "No" when he should have said "Yes,"
who sometimes whined and teased and cried
when a smile would have made everybody happy,
who let two hands do wrong instead of right,
who let two feet go THAT way instead of THIS way.
God calls all our badness sin.[3]
　　God couldn't let a child like that
into His lovely heavenly home.

God loved you.
He wanted you to be happy.
And so He made a plan for you . . .
a plan so wonderful, a plan so marvelous,
that only God could think of it![4]

[2] John 1:12
[3] Romans 3:23
[4] Romans 6:23

God's Plan

God said, "Sin must be punished. That is right.
"If only someone would take the punishment for all
the sinners."

But who could it be?

It would have to be Someone who had never
sinned Himself.

It would have to be Someone who always did right.

It would have to be Someone who loves sinners very,
very much.

Who could there be with so much love for all sinners
that He would take their punishment . . .

    when HE was good,
    when HE did not sin,
    when HE always did right?

In all of heaven,
and on all the earth,
there was just one Person.

God's own Son, the Lord Jesus Christ.[1]

He said, "I love boys and girls and men
and women more than I love Myself.
I will leave My beautiful heavenly home.
I will take the punishment for their sin."

[1]Hebrews 4:15

7

And He did. Jesus was born in Bethlehem, and laid in a
manger-bed. He grew to be a Child, just as you have.
Then He became a Man who went around helping everyone.
Jesus told people about God, His Father, who wanted to
be their heavenly Father.

Then it came time for Jesus Christ to suffer for our sins. Wicked people told terrible lies about Him. That hurt Him inside.

Wicked people beat Jesus, and nailed Him to a cross to die. That hurt His body.

But the worst hurt of all was that God, His Father, had to leave Him alone on the cross.

For Jesus had all our badness on Him then. Jesus took it all and made it His own . . .[2] " . . .who His own self bore our sins in His own body . . ."[3]

So God had to leave Jesus alone. And that was the worst hurt of all . . . such a BIG hurt that we cannot understand how terrible it was.

[2] 2 Corinthians 5:21
[3] 1 Peter 2:24

And NOW the sad part of the story is over!
Now the gladness makes us sing! After Jesus
had suffered and died, the punishment was over.
He came to life again in a wonderful new body
that nobody could hurt.

He went back to heaven to His loving Father
God, never to be separated from Him,
never to die. Jesus had made a way for us to
come to heaven to live. He had made a way
for us to belong to God's family.[4]

[4]1 Corinthians 15:3-4

Our Part

Jesus had done His part. And what an easy part ours is, compared with Jesus' hard part!

Our part is to know, "I'm a sinner. "I'm sorry for my sin. "Jesus died for me. "I want Jesus' punishment to count for me."
Our part is to say, and mean it with all our heart, "Dear God, I want Jesus to save me from being punished for my sin. I want Him for my Saviour now. Amen."

11

God says in John 3:16:

"For God so loved the world" . . . that means you;
"that He gave His only
begotten Son". . . . . that means the Lord Jesus
Christ;

"that whosoever believeth
in Him: . . . . that's what you did when you
asked Him to save you from
your sin;

"should not perish". . . . . or be punished for all your
sins;

"but have everlasting life." . . . and that's living with God
in heaven forever and ever.

What Happened

What happened? Perhaps more than you even know!
Yes, Jesus took away your sin.[1] Maybe you felt all clean
and happy inside. Sometimes people do. Maybe
you didn't feel any different. Sometimes people
don't feel different.

What else happened? You became a member
of God's family right that very moment. Because
Jesus is your Saviour, God is your heavenly Father, and
He will always love you. He will always care
for you. He will always help you.

Don't you feel happy way down deep inside,
just thinking about it? Every time you feel sad,
read again what happened when you asked Jesus
to be your Saviour.

---

[1] 2 Corinthians 5:17

How God's Children Grow

We've talked about how you got into God's family–
The best family of all. Now you're ready to learn how
God's children grow.

When you were a little new baby, your family loved
you . . . and they wanted you to grow.

Now that you've just come into God's family, you're a new
Christian—a baby one. Even grown men and women who
become Christians are baby Christians at first. It's a very happy
time when you're a new Christian.

But of course you want to grow.[1] You don't want to stay a
baby Christian for years and years.

How does a Christian grow? Let's find out.

[1] 2 Peter 3:18

Growing by Talking

One important way of growing is to pray—to talk to God. God's child needs to talk to his Father every day. And that's just what a new Christian wants to do!

You can tell your loving Father about all your fun. You can tell Him about your sad times.

You can thank God for loving you and for all His good gifts.

You can ask God for help. God is always ready to listen.[1]

When will you talk to God? Anytime, of course. Because He is God, He is never too busy. Because He is God, He even hears a prayer you think.

[1]Philippians 4:6

But one of the best times to pray is when you wake up in the morning. You can start the day with God. You can thank Him for taking care of you all night. You can ask Him for His help during the day.

You can ask God to remind you of the way His child should act. Ask Him to help you remember Bible verses in which He tells you what is right.

Do you know "Children, obey your parents in the Lord,"[2]
"Be ye kind, one to another"?[3]

You will need God's help to obey these commands.

Morning is a good time to pray.

[2]Ephesians 6:1
[3]Ephesians 4:32a

But morning is not the only time to pray.

You will want to thank God for your food. Without food you would get thin and weak and die. God made the food grow.

We should remember and thank Him.

We can thank Him with a prayer-poem.
"For all we eat,
For all we wear,
For all we have everywhere,
We thank You, heavenly Father."

We can thank Him with our own words.

We can thank Him aloud, or whisper quietly.

Perhaps we can sing a thank-You song. Do you know one?

There are many ways to give thanks to God.

Besides morning and mealtime, you can pray anytime.

You'll want to thank God when you see something lovely He has made.

You'll want to thank Him for His good gifts to you, such as your strong legs that run, your ten fingers, your two arms.

God says, "It is a good thing to give thanks."[4]

We can say, "I will praise You with my whole heart."[5] That is thanking Him with Bible words.

18

[4]Psalm 92:1
[5]Psalm 138:1

And then there will be times when you need help.
You can whisper, "Father, help me to obey."

"Father, help me to be kind."

What could be better than to have God Himself
always with you, ready to listen?[6]

God's child grows by praying.

[6]Hebrews 13:5b

Growing by Listening

God's child grows by talking to God.

God's child grows by listening to God. You wouldn't enjoy a friend who always talked to you but never let you talk, would you?

God has very important things to say to you.

Where does God say these important things? In His world, yes . . . we can hear Him if we know how to listen . . . [1]
The tall trees say that God is strong. The pretty flowers say that God is good to make such loveliness. The tiny birds who fly so high say God is wise.

20

But God says much, much more
to you in another place. In the Bible,
God tells you all the important things
He wants you to know.[2]
He tells you why He made you.
He tells you what He wants you to do.
He tells you what to love and what
to hate.
He tells you what He is like.
And as you read more and more
about Him, you will love Him more
and more. As you read what He has
done, you will understand more
about His ways. You
will feel more a part
of His family, and
you will act more like
His child every day.

[2] 2 Timothy 3:16-17

People who can read well, read the Bible every day so they can be growing Christians. But perhaps you can't read well enough yet to read the Bible. Or perhaps you haven't learned to read at all. You want to be a growing Christian. What can you do?

First of all, you can plan. Yes, you can plan to read the Bible every day after you learn to read.

But what about now?

Perhaps you can read easier books than the Bible. Then you can read a book of Bible stories. Every day you can read a story. You can look for something new each time you read a story. You can see if you know the whole story without reading it.

You can pretend you are a missionary to other boys and girls. You can tell them the Bible story. Then read it again to be sure you have it right.

If you can read a little bit, you can
read your Sunday School paper,
read the Bible story over and over till you know it well,
read the Bible verse in your Sunday School paper,
read it over each day of the week by yourself,
think about it.

If you don't know how to read at all, what can you do?
You can ask someone at home, or an older friend to read a book
of Bible stories to you, or read your Sunday School paper or
workbook to you, or read a Bible verse to you from your Sunday
School paper.

You can be a growing Christian.

If you can or if you cannot read,
you can have a VERY special time each day
when you think about God,
when you remember what you learned in Sunday School,
and you talk to God about it.

Then you can think about what God has done and what He wants you to do. You can say the Bible verse over each day. You can pray about it.

When you pray, you can ask God to help you remember and obey the Bible verse.

Then you will be living as God's child.

And you will be a growing Christian.

Growing by Doing

So, growing Christians pray and read God's message to them. They are quiet when they talk to God. They are quiet when they listen to Him.

Are they quiet all day?

OF COURSE NOT!

Christians grow by doing things for God too.[1]

[1]Ephesians 2:10

How can you use your legs for God?
    Can you run an errand
for Mother or Father?
    Can you get things?
    Can you take things back?
    Can you go quickly . . . even
if you'd rather play?
    Your legs can show that
you are God's child.

How can you use
your arms for Him?
    Can you carry
something to somebody?
    Can you give . . .
and not grab?
    Can your hands make
other people smile . . .
and not frown or cry?
    Your arms can show
that you are God's child.

How can you use your voice for Him?

Can you say "Yes" when that's what Mother wants to hear?

Can you say "No" when that's the right answer?

Can you sing and not whine, and keep still and not quarrel?

When it's hard to tell the truth exactly, can you let the Lord help you do it?

Your voice can show that you are God's child.

How can you use your mind for Him?

When Mother or Father isn't with you, can you think of the right way to act and speak . . . and do it?

When someone tries to get you to do wrong, can you think what Jesus would want you to do . . . and do it?

Your thinking can show that you are God's child.

God's work makes us happy, and it makes other people happy too.

A Christian grows when he works for God.

Going on Growing

But do God's children ever make mistakes? Can they ever sin?

Yes . . . they sometimes do.

Sometimes they forget to ask the Lord's help in the morning . . . and they may forget to talk to Him all day long.

Sometimes it seems so easy to do wrong . . . and they don't let the Lord be their Helper.

Sometimes they seem to forget that the Lord is with them! And they sin.

"What happens then?" you ask. "Does God stop loving them?"

No, God never stops loving His children.
But He cannot make them happy if they disobey Him.
He cannot make them feel like singing all day.

 If one of God's children sins, he is not happy.
He doesn't feel like talking to his heavenly Father.
He doesn't feel like listening to God.

 He feels like running away from God and hiding.

And he should run. He should run to God quickly and say,
 "O God, I'm sorry.
 I have done wrong.
 I never want to do that wrong again.
 Please forgive me, for Jesus' sake."

And what do you think happens then?
God remembers that Jesus died for that child's sin.
God sees that the child is truly sorry and doesn't want to sin.
God forgives the sin for Jesus' sake.[1]
And all at once, God's child is happy again.
He can sing. He can pray. He can do things for God.
He can go on growing as a Christian.

Isn't it WONDERFUL to be God's child?
Let's thank Him again, right now.

[1] 1 John 1:9; 2:1